Bristol Radical Pamphleteer #45

Mabel Tothill

Feminist, socialist, pacifist

June Hannam

ISBN 978-1-911522-48-5

Bristol Radical History Group. 2019.
www.brh.org.uk
brh@brh.org.uk

Contents

Acknowledgements

I am grateful to Jeremy Clarke, Cyril Pearce, Moira Martin and Helen Meller for their generosity in sharing their research findings with me. Many thanks to Dawn Dyer who has given so much of her time to help me locate sources for Mabel Tothill and also for suggesting many of the illustrations used in this pamphlet. Thanks also to Roger Sturge for information about his family and to Linda Watts for researching details of the lives of Elizabeth and Gertrude Giles.

Illustrations

For permission to use pictures from Bristol Central Reference Library please contact refandinfo@bristol.gov.uk.

Introduction

Mabel Tothill was born into a comfortable, middle-class family, but was to become a socialist, an advocate for conscientious objectors and a Labour councillor. How can we explain her political and personal journey? Her choices were very much her own but she was certainly not unique. Many other women of her class and generation, influenced by a growing concern with poverty and work conditions in the late nineteenth century, were attracted to the labour movement. Strikes among less skilled workers, new unionism and the revival of socialism in the 1880s and 90s opened up different spaces for middle-class women to take action and offered new solutions to the social problems that they encountered.

Influenced by the nineteenth-century women's rights movement, they not only sought to improve the lives of the working class as a whole, but also highlighted the specific needs and interests of women. Along with working-class women activists they raised issues about gender inequalities in the workplace, in the home and within the labour movement itself; they pointed to the lack of representation of women in labour organisations and debated whether there should be separate spaces for women within socialist and labour groups; whether birth control and domestic questions were political issues and, most significant of all in this period, whether priority should be given to women's suffrage.

Women made different decisions about political priorities and how to tackle gender inequalities. They also shifted their position over time as the political context changed. An in-depth look at the lives of individual women, in particular those who are less well known, is one way to build an understanding of the complexities of political choices made in this period. It also sheds light on the specific features of local socialist and labour groups and helps to explain their appeal.[1] Biographies of a wide range of socialist women have moved us away from an emphasis on a small group of national propagandists, revealing the variety of ways in which women engaged with

---

1 Sandra Stanley Holton, for example, suggested that a biographical approach could provide a more complex and nuanced account of the campaign for women's suffrage. She looked at the careers of several lesser known women suffrage campaigners to demonstrate 'the complex cross-currents within the movement that could not be successfully explored simply by adopting the labels "bourgeois", "working-class", "liberal", "radical", "socialist" or "conservative" or by a resort to the supposedly simple militant/constitutionalist dichotomy'. 'Challenging masculinism: personal history and microhistory in feminist studies of the women's suffrage movement', *Women's History Review*, 20,5 (2011), p. 836. S.S. Holton, *Suffrage Days: Stories from the Women's Suffrage Movement* (London, Routledge: 1996). See also J. Liddington, *Rebel Girls: Their Fight for the Vote* (London, Virago: 2006).

socialist politics, in particular at a local level.[2] They have enabled us to gain new insights into both the socialist and the feminist movements and the complex interactions between them. They have also shown that there was no simple definition of what it meant to be a socialist feminist or indeed what it meant to be a feminist or to be woman-centred and engaged in socialist politics.[3]

Mabel Tothill was primarily a local activist. Her life story can shed light on the specific characteristics of suffrage, socialist and peace politics in Bristol in those heady days of social upheaval before, during and immediately after the First World War. This is not a full blown biography – partly because the evidence for her life is patchy, but also because she did not act alone. She was always part of networks of activists, sometimes separate from each other and sometimes overlapping. So this pamphlet is as much about a set of events, and the behaviour of a group of friends and comrades around those events, as it is about one woman's life story.[4]

Early Life

Mabel Caroline Tothill was born in Liverpool in 1869. She had one older sibling, Gertrude Fanny who was born in 1865. The sisters moved with their parents, Charles Waring William Tothill and Lucy Fanny, née Curtis, to Hull where their father was manager of the Starch Blue and Black Lead factory.[5] By 1892 the two sisters had moved to Bristol and were resident at 19 Beaconsfield Road. They may have been attracted to the city because their father came from Bristol and still had relatives there. Mabel's unmarried aunt, Emily Tothill, for example, lived a few doors away in Beaconsfield Road.[6] Mabel had also attended Clifton High School as a teenager and still had friends there from her school days.[7]

2 For example, see J. Hannam, *Isabella Ford, 1855-1924* (Oxford, Blackwell: 1989); K. Hunt, 'Dora Montefiore: a different communist', in *Party People, Communist Lives: Explorations in Biography*. K. Morgan, J. McIlroy, A.Campbell (Eds) (London, Lawrence and Wishart: 2001). J. Liddington, *The Life and Times of a Respectable Rebel. Selina Cooper 1864-1946* (London, Virago: 1984); A. Stout, *Phoebe Cusden of Reading* (Reading, Reading Dusseldorf Association: 1997); C. Steedman, *Childhood, Culture and Class in Britain: Margaret McMillan, 1860-1931* (London, Virago: 1990).

3 For a discussion of these issues see J. Hannam and K. Hunt, *Socialist Women: Britain 1880s-1920s* (London, Routledge: 2002), chapter 2.

4 Holton,'Challenging masculinism', p.837.

5 1871 and 1881 Census. Fanny Curtis was born in Staines, the daughter of a surgeon. They were married in 1861.

6 Kelly's Directory 1892-1911 (Bristol Reference Library).

7 A.F.Tod , 'C.H.S. Working Girls Club 1895-1927', in Anon, *The Jubilee Book of the Clifton High School 1877-1927* (Bristol, A. W. Ford: 1927), pp.114-15.

Four years later, in 1896, Mabel's parents also moved to Bristol when her father retired. Although Lucy Tothill died in the same year, Charles continued to live separately from his daughters at 1 Cambridge Park, Redland, supported by two servants, a housemaid and a cook. At the time of the 1901 census Gertrude and Mabel were recorded as staying with their father. This did not appear to be a permanent arrangement, however, since they were still separately listed in their own home in the local directory until 1906. After this date, Charles Tothill moved to a bigger house at 123 Pembroke Road, Clifton, which had 13 rooms and an extra servant, a parlour maid. It is likely that his health was failing but it is unclear whether his daughters moved in with him before his death in 1910. Gertrude was listed as resident in his house in the 1911 census and continued to live at that address for most of her life.[8]

Mabel, who was brought up as an Anglican, had already shown her independence of mind in joining the Society of Friends and also the Bristol branch of the National Union of Women's Suffrage Societies (NUWSS). She is one of a small number of women singled out as key leaders and active workers in the suffrage cause in Bristol although she was not a committee member or office holder in the local branch.[9]

Quaker friendship networks

Some middle-class women were drawn to socialism after becoming involved in strikes and trade union organisation. For others it was because of an interest in social welfare. This was certainly the case for Mabel. Throughout her life she was committed to the idea of personal social service. Bristol provided an ideal environment for her work. From its inception in the late 1870s the University of Bristol had had a reputation for taking an interest in social problems and according to Helen Meller, ideas about social service 'were alive in the city'.[10] It was a time when middle-class men and women were searching for ways to prevent poverty and to link voluntary work with local authority initiatives. When she lived in Hull Mabel had organised children's classes and girls' clubs and promoted the establishment of libraries.[11]

On her arrival in Bristol she became part of a network of women and men who were committed to promoting educational opportunities for all,

8 1911 census.
9 A.M.Beddoe, *The Early Years of the Women's Suffrage Movement* (Bradford on Avon, The Library Press: 1911), p.6.
10 H. Meller, ' How to live in the modern city: women's contribution to Bristol 1860s to 1930s', 2017 Joe Bettey Lecture, ALHA *Newsletter,* 153, January to April (2018), p.3.
11 'Councillor Mabel Tothill', Bristol's Public Men and Women no.26, *Bristol Times and Mirror*, 23 August 1921.

Marian Pease, 1912.

to undertaking practical work to mitigate the effects of poverty and to researching social problems. Quakers in particular were inspired by the decision of the Society of Friends Annual meeting in 1895 to look outward and to become engaged with contemporary social questions. Marian Pease was a key figure in this Bristol group and became a close personal friend. She came from a Quaker family steeped in ideals of public service. Her father Thomas Pease was one of the proprietors of the Great Western Cotton Factory and chairman of the Board of Guardians, while her brother Edward was a founder of the Fabian Society. One sister, Rosa, became the first female chair of the Board of Guardians in 1920 while another sister, Dora, was the first president of the Bristol branch of the Women's Co-operative Guild, established in 1890.[12]

Marian Pease set up a Cotton Girls Club in Barton Hill in 1880. Mabel Tothill helped her friend with the club where she gained first-hand experience of the lives of working-class girls and young women. She might have been introduced to this when she was at school in Bristol since Marian Pease was involved with pupils at the Clifton High School for Girls and encouraged them to take an interest in social questions. Marian Pease and Mabel Tothill shared a commitment to expanding educational opportunities for all. The movement for higher and secondary education for women and girls brought together women from leading Quaker families in Bristol, including the Sturges and the Peases, who were later to become involved in campaigns for women's suffrage and peace.[13]

Marian Pease had been one of the first women to obtain a bursary from the Clifton Association for the Higher Education of Women to study at degree level at University College, Bristol, which was open to women as

12 E. Jackson, *Industrial Co-operation in Bristol: A Study in Democracy* (Manchester, CWS: 1911), p.514.
13 M. Martin, 'Guardians of the poor: a philanthropic female elite in Bristol', *Regional Historian*, 9, summer (2002), p.3.

Berkeley Square, by Samuel Loxton, 1918.

well as men. She was appointed as Mistress of Method when the University established a Day Training College for women in Berkeley Square in 1892, a post she held for twenty years.[14] She was also president of the Bristol Pupil Teachers' Association, founded in 1894. Its aim was to help pupil teachers to make best use of their limited spare time by organising recreation and encouraging general reading.[15]

Mabel was a visitor to elementary schools in the 1890s and was involved in the Workers' Education Association (WEA) and in Adult Schools throughout her life. Adult Schools were associated with the Society of Friends and were important for the development of the Independent Labour Party (ILP) in Bristol. Participation in the Adult Schools was at a peak in the decade before the First World War. The Schools offered classes, discussion groups and study circles at weekends and in the evenings.

14 *Clifton Society*, 21 November 1912. Marian Pease was in charge of the College. Her title Mistress of Method referred to the practical aspects of teaching.
15 Report of Bristol Pupil Teachers' Association, 1894. BRL3.3936.

Personal social service:
the Charity Organisation Society and the Civic League

When she arrived in Bristol Mabel also became active in the Charity Organisation Society (COS). By the late 1890s she was joint honorary secretary of the Bristol branch.[16] At first this might seem surprising since the COS had a reputation for taking a harsh view of the poor. On the other hand the Society did attempt to develop new ideas through a 'scientific' approach to poverty. COS members criticised almsgiving when there was no attempt to distinguish between the deserving and the undeserving poor. It was argued that only a systematic approach would prevent poverty and reduce the need for poor relief. It was these ideas that inspired women such as Mabel Tothill. She claimed that the COS 'aims to prevent distress in such a thorough way it will not recur'.[17] Similarly Elizabeth Sturge, also joint honorary secretary of the Bristol branch, later claimed that she had been attracted by the more systematic approach encapsulated by the COS.[18] On behalf of the Bristol branch, for example, Mabel signed an advertisement in the *Western Daily Press* for funds to help a 67 year old painter who had led an industrious life. He had used up his savings to help his sick wife and the Society hoped to be able to pay him 7/6 a week for six months to get him on his feet so that he could become self- supporting.[19]

Mabel might also have been attracted to the Bristol COS because it provided a congenial space for women to take active roles. Many of those involved were Quakers who were part of her social and friendship networks. In 1896, for example, Norah Fry was honorary assistant secretary and was followed by Elizabeth Sturge. In 1908, after local authorities had been given greater responsibility for social welfare, the COS amalgamated with the Bristol League of Personal Service and Public Welfare to form the Bristol Civic League. Again women played key roles in the League. Miss A. T. Thompson was secretary and both Mabel Tothill and Fanny Marian Townsend compiled important reports on the League's work. The aim of the League was to promote public welfare by means of public service and to provide trained and experienced visitors to help local authorities. This was entirely in keeping with Mabel Tothill's outlook.

---

16 *Western Daily Press (WDP)*, 8 February 1898.
17 Bristol and Somerset Quarterly Meeting. Committee on Social Services, Report by Mabel Tothill, 1908, Friends Library, L18/06, p.5.
18 E. Sturge, *Reminiscences of My Life* (privately printed: 1928), pp.54-5.
19 *WDP*, 8 February 1898.

Working class housing in St James, by Samuel Loxton, 1913.

Central to her approach to poverty was the importance of personal contact with the poor through visiting their homes. As early as 1905, Mabel had supported a proposal to form a local Guild of Friendly Visitors under the auspices of the COS. She argued that the Society already helped to administer the Poor Law in Bristol but fell short on personal visiting. She was critical of visitors giving money when their sympathies were aroused, but thought instead that their task should be to work with people in their homes and to give advice. The rich and poor had many things in common and 'as a matter of personal experience the visitors would find that in the work there was fellowship'.[20] Her use of the word fellowship is an interesting one. If it is defined as a feeling of friendship that people have when they join together in a community of interest to get things done, then it can be seen as something that was central to her social activism, including her settlement work and her socialist politics.

Mabel compiled two reports on the subject of personal contact with the poor. One was for the Committee on Social Services of the Bristol and Somerset Quarterly Meeting (Society of Friends). She conducted a survey of the extent to which members of local Meetings were involved in social questions and emphasised the importance of preventative work. She argued that this could largely be achieved by influencing individual character, especially that of children, as well as providing material assistance. In the context of the School Feeding Act and the Medical Inspection Act she believed that home visits should be made to encourage parents to feed their children properly and to maintain a healthy environment. Visitors would need to be well trained.[21] Mabel pointed out that the University of Birmingham offered a one year course leading to a diploma and that practical experience could be gained through work with the COS or with Adult Schools and Girls Clubs.

She made similar points in a second, lengthy report, undertaken on behalf of the Civic League. Here she underlined the importance of voluntary groups working closely with local authorities and the necessity of providing training for volunteers.[22] This was published in 1914. She gave a systematic account of her views in an address given over a decade later entitled 'the relation of personal devotion to social service'. Here she suggested that social service implied two things- dealing with the system of society and also with the individual people who composed it. She claimed that there was 'no form of work that was not affected by the personality of the worker'. Her approach as a Quaker underpinned her arguments since she thought that prayer from the depths of the soul, made impulsively at the right moment, was worth far more than organised, formal prayer in dealing with social questions.[23]

20 *WDP*, 3 November 1905.
21 Bristol and Somerset Quarterly Meeting, Committee on Social Services, Report.
22 *WDP*, 2 February 1915.
23 *WDP*, 4 January 1924.

Barton Hill Settlement

Mabel's interest in education, in gaining experience of workers' lives and in preventing social problems came together in 1911 in a new venture, the Barton Hill University Settlement. It is likely that she was drawn into this by her friend Marian Pease who, along with Hilda Cashmore, was the driving force behind the development of the Settlement. In 1904 Marian Pease had appointed Hilda Cashmore to the post of history tutor at the Day Training College and the two women encouraged students to join a 'social service guild'.[24] They were described as 'forward looking and open to new ideas, and both deeply concerned with individuals and with social problems', a description that could equally have been applied to Mabel.[25]

The Settlement movement had developed from the 1880s when Samuel Barnett and Benjamin Jowett founded Toynbee Hall in London's East End. The intention was to encourage male university students to gain experience of working-class life and to study broad political problems such as poverty. Women became more involved in Settlement work after the turn of the century. Many sought to develop a different approach and took inspiration from Jane Addams who founded Hull House in Chicago. She aimed to create a community of university women who would undertake research into social problems and work with the community and the labour movement to achieve reforms. This approach was in tune with that of Hilda Cashmore who did not agree 'that only the rich could teach the poor to improve their lives'.[26] She thought that settlement workers should be pledged to 'create an atmosphere so alive, and yet so patient of difference, that a meeting ground is made for men and women of various classes and of conflicting views, a place for free discussion and the birth of new ideas'.[27]

This was not at all easy to achieve. Hilda Jennings recalled that: 'naturally some fears of the motives and methods of the Settlement were expressed. To some, its philosophy appeared strangely foreign to the conception of working-class solidarity and "class" struggle'.[28] Nonetheless the residents made great efforts to gain the trust of the local community. The Settlement promoted the general welfare of the local neighbourhood through the provision of clubs for girls and boys and offered educational classes on a range of subjects for all

24 H. Jennings, *University Settlement Bristol: 50 years of Change, 1911-71* (Bristol, University of Bristol Settlement Community Association:1971), p.5.

25 Jennings, *University Settlement Bristol* (1971), p.5.

26 Meller, 'How to live in the modern city', p.3.

27 Jennings, *University Settlement* (1971), p.6.

28 H. Jennings, *University Settlement Bristol: Fifty Years of Change, 1911-1961* (Bristol, University of Bristol Settlement Community Association:1961), p.10.

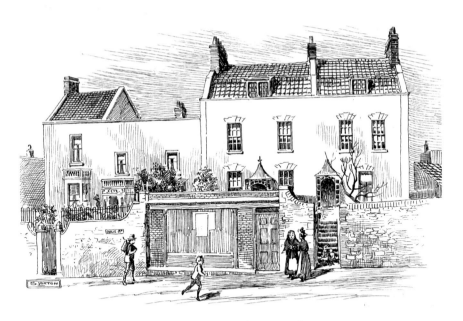

Barton Hill Settlement, by Samuel Loxton.

who were interested. The emphasis on education meant that there were strong links with the National Union of Teachers and the Workers' Educational Association. George Leonard, president of the WEA, was professor of history at the University and taught many of the classes at the Settlement. Bristol University worked closely with the Settlement to offer the systematic study of social and industrial problems and to provide training in social work. This fulfilled one of Hilda Cashmore's aims–to expand professional employment opportunities for women.

East Bristol was chosen as the location of the Settlement since it was a solid working-class district and one that both Marian Pease and Mabel Tothill already knew well. Mabel, for instance, was the honorary secretary of the East Bristol branch of the Civic League. She became one of the first residents at the Settlement along with Hilda Cashmore, the first warden, and Lettice Jowitt, a university lecturer, also from the Day Training College. All three were Quakers. Walter Hennessey, later to become a Labour alderman, took a course of economics lectures at the Settlement in 1911. He described the three residents, along with Marian Pease, as 'a very powerful team of organisers, unequalled in their strength of character, the determination of their attack upon ignorance and squalid home life and in their untiring efforts to help by organising the various classes of men, women and children and by visiting the homes for a few minutes social chat'.[29]

Nonetheless it was difficult to start with. '"How shall we start making friends with our neighbours?" asked Miss Tothill. The answer [from Hilda Cashmore] was characteristic. "You and I both love children. We will start with them"'[30] Mabel helped with the children's clubs, taught a literature class and visited local homes. She also provided much needed finance for the Settlement, having been left a legacy by her aunt and then almost £65,000 by her father, which was shared with her sister.[31] While fund raising and public donations enabled the Settlement to be established, it needed more funding in order to expand. As well as donating money to get the Settlement off the ground, Mabel later bought the large garden and substantial house at 63 Barton Hill Road to be the headquarters for a Boys' Club and open air school to help children with tuberculosis. In 1919 she bought four more cottages and gave them to the Settlement, while Marian Pease made a gift of a house in the same year.[32]

It is not clear when Mabel first became attracted to socialist politics and to the Independent Labour Party. Mabel's work in the Settlement and the people that she met there must have predisposed her to take a stronger interest in the labour movement. Hilda Cashmore was a lifelong supporter of the Labour Party and of trade unionism. During the cotton workers' strike of 1912 she invited Margaret Bondfield, a trade union organiser, who had been sent from London to settle the strike, to stay at the Settlement. They had a different approach to the dispute. Hilda Cashmore thought the factory should be kept open despite paying low wages, because of its importance in the community, whereas Margaret Bondfield thought it should be closed. Hilda's view prevailed and Margaret Bondfield later observed that, although the factory closed down several years afterwards, 'the line taken by Hilda Cashmore and her colleagues wiped out much of the bitterness, and the Trade Unions and the Settlement worked together'.[33]

It is interesting to note that it was support for women's suffrage that appeared to be more controversial. In 1912, a major female subscriber to the Settlement from the Wills family threatened to withhold her subscription until she was assured that a rumour that Settlement residents were 'actively

29 W.H. Hennessey, 'Foreword', *The Magazine of the University Settlement*, Bristol, 5, Autumn (1950).

30 H. Jennings, *University Settlement* (1971), p.11.

31 *London Gazette*, 15 November 1904–Report of the death of Emily Tothill, spinster, 59 Beaconsfield Road. Mabel, her sister Gertrude and her father 'proved' the will.

32 University Settlement, Barton Hill, Annual Report July 1917-July 1919, BRL, B16643.

33 Jennings, *University Settlement* (1971), p. 16.

engaged in furthering women's suffrage in east Bristol' were false. Hilda Cashmore agreed that one resident, namely Mabel Tothill, was so engaged and wrote back that 'I can imagine no lady of any age and experience, living in a university settlement, who would care to be dictated to'.[34]

The Suffrage-Labour Alliance: Campaigning with the ILP in East Bristol

Women's suffrage provided another point of contact between Mabel and the ILP. The issue was widely discussed in East Bristol with talks on the subject being given at the Barton Hill Adult School. Mabel might well have been at the demonstration organised by the East Bristol ILP in favour of women's suffrage that was held at the Barton Hill baths in January 1912.[35] Walter and Bertha Ayles, with whom she worked closely just before the war, both attended the demonstration. Walter was the organising secretary of the Bristol ILP and was a city councillor, while his wife Bertha was a part-time organiser for the Women's Labour League (WLL) in the South West.

They were both keen supporters of the women's suffrage campaign. In 1913, for instance, Walter was one of many men who gave a speech at a Durdham Down meeting to support members of the NUWSS Suffrage Pilgrimage before they set off for London.[36] Mabel was also there and with Hilda Cashmore attended a special ceremony at St Stephen's Church where the vicar claimed that the church could give 'encouragement and blessing to such a desirable object as women's suffrage'.[37]

By the time of the Pilgrimage Mabel was certainly working closely with ILP members in East Bristol to promote women's suffrage. In 1912 the National Union of Women's Suffrage Societies, demoralised by the Liberal Government's handling of the suffrage issue, changed its strategy and agreed to form an alliance with the Labour Party. Some, such as Millicent Fawcett, saw this as a temporary expedient, whereas others, known as democratic

34 Correspondence between Miss E. Wills and Miss H. Cashmore, 3 September 1912, and reply from Hilda Cashmore to Miss Robinson (for Miss Wills), 7 Sept 1912, Bristol University Settlement Archive now lost; quoted in J.R. Harrow, 'The development of university settlements in England, 1884-1939', unpublished PhD, London School of Economics and Political Science, 1987, pp. 404-405.

35 Bristol ILP Branch minutes, 17 January 1912, University of Bristol Library Special Collections.

36 The NUWSS Pilgrimage was designed to give publicity to the cause using non-militant methods. Women walked from different parts of the country to converge on Hyde Park for a large rally in July 1913.

37 *Bristol Times and Mirror*, 16 July 1913.

Walter and Bertha Ayles, 1911.

suffragists, thought that there was a natural empathy between Labour and feminism and that the new arrangement would be permanent.[38] An Election Fighting Fund (EFF) was set up to support Labour candidates in selected seats where Liberals were hostile to women's suffrage. East Bristol was seen as a key target since the Liberal MP and Minister, Charles Hobhouse, was an active opponent of women's suffrage.

Annie Townley, a paid organiser for the EFF, the wife of a textile worker and member of the ILP, was sent to East Bristol to carry out election work

38 H. L. Smith, *The British Women's Suffrage Campaign, 1866-1926* (Harlow, Pearson Education: 1907, 2nd ed.), pp.63-4.

Park Street, location of NUWSS office, 1900.

on behalf of women's suffrage and the Labour Party. She was seen as such an effective propagandist that Margaret Robertson, one of the NUWSS organisers charged with suffrage work among miners, identified her as someone who should be sent to help convert them to women's suffrage since 'Mrs Townley would be good for *bad* miners'.[39] Finding that the Liberal dominated Bristol NUWSS branch was lukewarm about the new policy, she worked instead through a new group, the East Bristol Women's Suffrage Society. Mabel Tothill was secretary and then president of this Society and most of the active workers were drawn from the ILP. The aim was to carry out propaganda in favour of women's suffrage and the Labour candidate. To that end propaganda was targeted at working-class women and men, with support sought from a variety of labour organisations, including the Women's Cooperative Guild, trade union branches, the Trades Council and the Labour Representative Committee.[40]

39 Margaret Robertson to Catherine Marshall, 30 April 1913, quoted in J. Vellacott, *From Liberal to Labour with Women's Suffrage: The Story of Catherine Marshall* (Montreal and Kingston, McGill-Queen's University Press: 1993), p.300.
40 *Common Cause*, 3 October, 13 May 1913.

The East Bristol WSS opened a shop in Barrow Road, Barton Hill. Margaret Roberston, who oversaw the work of the EFF organisers, reported in the *Common Cause* that 'Many people call at the shop, and the talks carried on there and outside the works are probably as valuable as the meetings in the way of propaganda.'[41] Local working-class women helped in the shop and were involved in fund-raising and in carrying out registration work. The Society suffered financially but used socials to raise money, to attract new members and to bring active workers even closer together. Mabel certainly made friendships in this period with working-class activists that were to endure through the war years and beyond, including with Walter and Bertha Ayles, Annie Townley and Hannah Higgins. Hannah was the mother of two young girls and, with her husband Tommy, a coach painter, was active in the ILP. [42] She was a vice chair of the Bristol Women's Labour League and a committee member of the East Bristol WSS, delivering speeches on women's suffrage and giving recitals, most likely of poetry, at the socials.[43]

Mabel was able to develop her skills as a platform speaker and propagandist during this campaign. She gave many speeches on behalf of the East Bristol WSS, both in indoor meeting halls and at open-air meetings that were organised in the summer months.[44] In a lengthy speech to open the campaign, she called upon the government to redeem its pledges by 'immediately introducing a government measure for the enfranchisement of women'. As WSPU militancy escalated she was appalled, along with other NUWSS members, at any suggestion that the East Bristol WSS was associated with militant methods. When the *Western Daily Press* reported that a meeting at 2 Mile Hill, St Michael's, had been organised by the 'women's militant suffrage society' she wrote an indignant letter to the paper to point out that it had been organised by the East Bristol WSS 'which expressly declares itself to be non-militant'.[45]

By this stage she had come to see the cause of women and the cause of Labour as intertwined. She said she was there to support women's suffrage and the Labour candidate Frank Sheppard: 'in many cases the interests of women were closely allied with the interests of the Labour Party, and many of those things for which women were working the Labour Party were working for as well'.[46] She also believed that the campaign in East Bristol had both

41 *Common Cause*, 18 July 1912.
42 W.H.A. 'Tommy Higgins of Bristol', *Labour Leader*, 14 March 1914.
43 *WDP*, 16 January 1914.
44 *Common Cause*, 24 July 1914.
45 *WDP*, 21 February 1914.
46 *WDP*, 19 April 1913.

encouraged working-class women to take an interest in suffrage and had also boosted membership of both sexes in the Bristol East ILP.[47] This relationship then became even closer when, in 1914, Walter Ayles, known for his strong commitment to women's rights, replaced Frank Sheppard as the Labour candidate.

It is not surprising that Mabel was drawn to the Bristol ILP in this period, since the outlook of many of its members mirrored her own. The local ILP was closely linked to the growth of Adult Schools in the city and drew its inspiration from Christianity as much as from Marx. Walter Ayles, for example, approached his socialism through the framework of religion and, as a pacifist, disliked the idea of a class war as much as war between nations. He advocated public ownership but aimed to achieve social change through the ballot box.[48] Mabel also argued that war, and the issues raised by that, should not be isolated from other social problems : '" class war", although theoretically purely economic in character, is both the cause and effect of profound bitterness'. She went on to say that 'greed and pride of possession are rife amongst us, and … physical suffering and a high rate of mortality characterise our industrial conditions quite as much as they do the international war'.[49] This shared perspective was to become even stronger with the outbreak of the First World War which was a testing time for those who held pacifist views.

War and Relief Work

After the declaration of war in August 1914 active campaigning on behalf of women's suffrage and of labour politics became less pronounced. At first, in common with many other NUWSS members throughout the country, Mabel became involved in assisting women and girls who had lost their jobs at the start of the war. She helped to administer the Prince of Wales Relief Fund in Bristol and was honorary treasurer of the sub-committee dealing with female unemployment. The aim was to set up a centre to provide training in needlework and cookery and to give a small maintenance grant to those who attended.[50] Mabel visited other cities to see what training was available. In Manchester, for example, there

47 *Common Cause*, 23 January 1914.
48 J. Saville and B. Whitfield, 'Ayles, Walter Henry (1879-1953): Trade Unionist, Pacifist and Labour M.P.', in *Dictionary of Labour Biography Volume 5*, J. Saville and J. Bellamy (Eds) (Houndmills, Palgrave Macmillan: 1979).
49 M.C. Tothill, 'War and the Social Order', *The Friend*, 9 October 1914. This was a report on a conference held by the Society of Friends at LLandudno.
50 *WDP*, 25 September 1914.

was a scheme for making toys, but she thought that it would be difficult to start this up in Bristol since it would need specialist equipment and the appropriate technical knowledge.[51] In December an appeal was made for funds so that seamstresses could be employed to make garments for distressed men and women in Belgium and France. Forty women were employed from 'a highly respectable class who would not like to receive relief without making a return'.[52]

The East Bristol WSS was also involved in administering the Prince of Wales Fund. The committee was represented in all the wards in its area. The shop was used as headquarters in one ward and suffrage members and others sat there three days a week to receive applications for relief. It was decided that members and 'friends' would meet at the shop on Tuesday afternoons.[53] This scheme was carried on into 1915. Many of the 'friends' of the WSS were the wives of soldiers and sailors. It was decided, therefore, to open the shop one evening a week so it could be used for recreation and as a reading room. Political education was still high on the agenda. Mabel, who remained as president, noted that there would be autumn lectures on the map of Europe, food prices, economic housekeeping, war service for women, education and child labour and a special lecture from Miss Brodie on her experience as a Poor Law Guardian.[54]

It is interesting to note that the Bristol NUWSS branch had already established a Patriotic Club, to be chaired by Elizabeth Sturge, in order to offer a similar recreational space for the female relatives of servicemen. The honorary secretary of the branch, Mabel Cross, had come up with this initiative. From the start of the war she had been superintendent of a maternity centre in Bedminster, which had given her hands-on experience of working-class mothers.[55] Nonetheless, the two 'clubs' remained separate.

The war-time political truce meant that party political campaign meetings were no longer held, but Annie Townley still continued to spend time in the ILP office and carried on with registration work among voters. In 1915, however, the NUWSS executive no longer sanctioned this work

---

51 *WDP*, 8 October 1914.
52 Letter from Mabel Tothill to the *WDP*, 12 February 1915.
53 *Common Cause*, 25 September 1915. In an attempt to gain more support from working-class women the NUWSS adopted a Friends of Women's Suffrage scheme in 1912. Women were visited in their homes, were given reading material and could enrol to show their support. They were not fully paid up members with voting rights. E.Crawford, *The Women's Suffrage Movement: A Reference Guide* (London, UCL: 1999), p.233.
54 *Common Cause*, 1 October 1915.
55 *WDP*, 14 November 1914, 25 November 1914.

Bedminster Maternity Centre, by Samuel Loxton.

and threatened to withdraw support from the candidature of Walter Ayles.[56] Some executive members had never approved of the alliance with the Labour Party and used the new context of war to obtain a change in policy. Mabel Tothill, Annie Townley and Walter Ayles then rushed to London to meet

56 This paragraph is based on J. Vellacott, *Pacifists, Patriots and the Vote. The Erosion of Democratic Suffragism in Britain during the First World War* (Houndmills, Palgrave Macmillan: 2007), pp.105-7 and S.S. Holton, *Feminism and Democracy. Women's Suffrage and Reform Politics in Britain, 1900-1918* (Cambridge, Cambridge University Press: 1986), pp.140-141.

with Millicent Fawcett and other executive members to argue against this decision. Annie Townley reminded the meeting that Walter Ayles had only agreed to stand because he was promised financial backing. She spoke about his competence, his high standing with the trade unions and her belief that he would 'leap into popularity at the end of the war over industrial questions'.[57] Both Annie and Walter emphasised that all the trust that had been built up between the labour movement and the women's suffrage campaign would be undermined. Mabel added her support, arguing that the East Bristol WSS had been established on the basis of EFF policy and its whole existence was intertwined with the fortunes of the Labour candidate.[58]

No decision emerged from this meeting. Annie Townley left 'feeling awfully sick of the N.U.' and her assessment was that 'Mrs Fawcett was hopeless'.[59] She subsequently wrote to warn the NUWSS that the Bristol group was considering resigning. In the event an exception was made for Bristol and it was agreed that election aid would be given to Ayles. Elsewhere the EFF policy was suspended until the circumstances of the next general election were known. Mabel Tothill and Annie Townley continued to be involved with the East Bristol WSS throughout the war. Mabel was re-elected each year as president and Annie Townley took over pro tem as secretary in 1917. From early in 1915, however, peace work began to take up more of their time.

Peace Campaigning

Mabel Tothill, Annie Townley, Hannah Higgins, Walter and Bertha Ayles, along with many other Bristol ILP members, were committed to seeking a negotiated peace and a just post-war settlement. This was the official policy of the ILP. They were also strongly pacifist and opposed any attempts to introduce compulsory military service. When conscription finally became law they gave their support to conscientious objectors. Many activists in the NUWSS felt the same. Matters came to a head when some members of the executive supported the holding of a Women's Peace Congress at The Hague in April 1915. Differences of opinion were so great that those in favour of working for peace then resigned from the executive and joined a new group that came out of the Congress, the Women's International League (WIL).[60]

57 Vellacott, *Pacifists,* p105.
58 Holton, *Feminism and Democracy*, p.141.
59 Vellacott, *Pacifists*, p.107.
60 The group formed after The Hague Congress was called the International Committee of Women for Permanent Peace. In Britain it was named the Women's International League.

Its peace aims mirrored those of the ILP and other mixed-sex peace groups such as the Union for Democratic Control (UDC).[61]

Mabel was one of those NUWSS members who supported the holding of the Peace Congress. Here she was in tune with some other Bristol suffragists, including many of her Quaker friends. Despite suffering from influenza, she was moved to express her views publicly because of an article in the *Western Daily Press*. She thought this was full of misunderstandings about the Women's Peace Congress. In response she sent a letter to the paper signed by herself and three other Quaker suffragists–her close friend Marian Pease, Marianne Hill (Mrs Burrow Hill) and Mariabella Fry Junior. They denied the accusation made in the paper that the Congress had urged the allies to ask Germany for terms of peace. Instead they claimed that resolutions had been passed calling on the belligerent powers to state what their terms would be. Women at the Congress were looking for a 'just peace', not any old kind of peace, and a 'humane' not a German peace. They could not agree with Christabel Pankhurst's view that violence should be met with violence. On the contrary the views expressed at the Congress were carefully considered and based on deep rooted principles as delegates tried to find a better way forward.[62]

It was a few months later that her position on the war was to cause even more controversy for Mabel. Bristol University came under attack for being pro German. A petition was sent to the city council complaining of pacifist sympathies among the staff. These accusations were re-iterated by Dr Geraldine Hodgson in a letter to the press. Staff at the Barton Hill Settlement, including Mabel Tothill, were criticised for engaging in 'semi-secret peace activities'.[63] The *Evening Times and Echo* , under the heading 'Pacifist Intrigue: Bristol University and the Pacifists', listed branches of the Fellowship of Reconciliation, one of which was 'M. C. Tothill, University Settlement, Barton Hill'. Included in a broader list of members of the Fellowship was Constance Gostrick who was also associated with the Settlement.[64]

61 For NUWSS differences on the war, see Vellacott, *Pacifists;* A. Wiltsher, *Most Dangerous Women: Feminist Peace Campaigners of the Great War* (London, Pandora: 1983). For an account of ILP attitudes, see K. Laysbourn, *The Rise of Socialism in Britain* (Stroud, Sutton: 1997), pp. 74-78; C. Pearce, *Comrades in Conscience. The Story of an English Community's Opposition to the Great War* (London, Francis Boutle Publishers, revised edition: 2014); T. Jowitt and K. Laybourn, 'War and socialism: the experience of the Bradford ILP 1914-18', in the *Centennial History of the Independent Labour Party*. D. James, T. Jowitt and K. Laybourn (Eds) (Halifax, Ryburn: 1992).

62 *WDP*, 20 April 1915.

63 *Bristol Times and Mirror*, 30 August 1915, 1 and 4 September 1915.

64 *Evening Times and Echo*, 28 August 1915 in a folder of cuttings, Bristol Record Office (BRO), DM526/6.

The Fellowship of Reconciliation, a non-denominational group, had been formed at the beginning of the war to bring together Christian pacifists who believed in non-violent resistance to war. Mabel Tothill and Walter Ayles were both members of the group and by 1915 Mabel was secretary of the Bristol branch. She had used Settlement notepaper, with her home address, to write a letter on behalf of the Fellowship. When the editor of the *Western Daily Press* contacted her about all of these allegations she denied any connection with the university itself, apologised for using Settlement notepaper and assured the editor that she had never carried out peace work among the women and girls at the Settlement.

Interestingly the editor accepted her word on this and wrote positively about the work that she had done for the Prince of Wales Fund. He also made a distinction between the Fellowship, which had never told young men not to fight, and the UDC which was less religious and far more political. Mabel had long been explicit about her pacifist views. In the far more difficult context of war, however, she did feel the need to sever her connections with the Settlement in order to protect her friend Hilda Cashmore and the on-going work of the Settlement itself. After a short time living with her sister in Pembroke Road, she moved into 27 Rosemary Street which was to be her home until the early 1920s.

From this point Mabel concentrated her efforts on promoting peace and, as Cyril Pearce points out, was 'at the centre of Bristol's anti-war community'.[65] Peace activism brought together socialists, liberal radicals, members of the Society of Friends and some members of the women's movement, many of whom had already worked together in the cause of women's suffrage before the war. As a middle–class Quaker who had been involved in a variety of groups and campaigns Mabel was well placed to make connections between these different strands. Many of the women had already formed strong friendships with each other, and with some men, before the war. In the difficult context of war, when their views were often vilified, these friendships became even stronger and new ones were developed. As Alison Ronan suggests, 'war, friendship and politics were deeply interlinked'. Anti-war campaigners often shared a commitment to 'social justice and the moral force of reason' which was the basis for friendships which they then relied upon for encouragement and support.[66]

---

65 C. Pearce, 'Indentifying war resister communities in Britain during the First World War', paper supplied by the author, November 2018.
66 A. Ronan, 'Fractured, fragile, creative: a brief analysis of wartime friendships between provincial women anti-war activists, 1914-1918', *North West Labour History*, 37 (2012-13), pp. 24, 27.

Mabel Tothill, Annie Townley, Hannah Higgins and other ILP socialists used a variety of different organisations in which to get their message across. Some were women-only spaces. For example, they joined with Quaker friends from the NUWSS, including Elizabeth and Helen Sturge, Marian Pease and members of the Fry family, in forming a Bristol branch of the Women's International League. Mabel was perhaps more at home here, given her class background and friendship with Marian Pease and the Sturge sisters. She took an active role, attending the national conference of the Women's International League in London in 1916 where she reported on the progress of the peace movement in Bristol. By the following year membership of the branch had risen from 60 to 84 members.[67]

Annie Townley and Hannah Higgins put more of their energies into the Women's Labour League, with Annie acting as president of the Bristol branch in 1916. Both women attended the League's annual conference held in Bristol in that year. They spoke of the need for the WLL to put pressure on the Labour Party to do something more active to promote peace.[68] Annie Townley also continued to monitor and take action on women's work and wages, speaking at meetings and writing articles in the ILP newspaper *Bristol Forward*.

ILP women also took part in mixed-sex peace organisations including the Union of Democratic Control and the No Conscription Fellowship (NCF). Mabel became chair, with Francis Radley as secretary, of the Bristol Peace Council. This was a broad front coalition bringing together ILP members and Christian pacifists opposed to war. It held conferences that were attended by Annie Townley and her husband Ernest, while Ernest was sent as a delegate to the Council on behalf of the ILP.[69]

Although groups such as the WIL, the UDC and the ILP did not seek to actively disrupt the war effort, they encountered considerable hostility and could find it difficult to rent premises in which to meet. Towards the end of 1915 the ILP planned to hold a demonstration at the Bristol Empire, Old Market. After opposition from the Lord Mayor and others, permission to use the venue was withdrawn by the manager. In November 1916, a planned meeting of the WIL could not take place since the Ladies Club Clifton decided that its rooms were not to be used for peace propaganda meetings.[70]

67 Women's International League, Annual Reports, 1916, 1917.
68 Women's Labour League, Annual Report, 1916.
69 Bristol ILP Branch Minutes, 4 October 1916.
70 *WDP*, 2 December 1915 and 28 November 1916.

Supporting Conscientious Objectors

In 1916 there was a shift in the focus of Mabel Tothill's peace work. The introduction of conscription led her to concentrate her efforts on supporting Bristol's conscientious objectors. Both Mabel and Walter Ayles had deep seated religious convictions that underpinned their opposition to conscription. Walter Ayles was an executive member of the No Conscription Fellowship and was arrested in early 1916, along with other executive members, for distributing a leaflet which called for the repeal of the Military Service Act. He was sentenced to 112 days imprisonment with hard labour at Pentonville. Later in the year he was imprisoned again when he was denied absolute exemption from military service and refused, instead, to take up work of national importance. In his appearance before the Bristol Crown Court in November he explained his Christian pacifist position.[71] He argued that there was a higher duty than to King and country and that was to humanity, to conscience and to God, and he claimed that all human life was sacred.[72]

Mabel Tothill held very similar views. She was opposed to militarism in all its forms, believed that human life was sacred and argued that men must have freedom of conscience. 'We have always believed England to be the "land of liberty". It is true that we have amongst us the downtrodden, the hungry, the sweated worker, yet a great majority undoubtedly have enjoyed a large measure of liberty of thought, speech and action'. She feared, though, that the nation had 'gone back to the methods of the Stuarts in her dealings with those who cannot conform....it is for us to see that the civil and religious liberties of our country are not further infringed, that her standards of right and wrong are not lowered, and that the God implanted guide in man which men call conscience is not scorned and put to shame'.[73]

Mabel believed that the conduct of individuals was as important as that of states. She argued that all men and women should recognise the self-interest, love of power and unrighteous anger that was within every one of them and that they should strive to express a 'higher spiritual ideal' in their everyday lives. She praised those who refused to fight and insisted that they should be described as patriotic since their devotion to peace meant they were 'animated by a no less deep love of country than those whose courage and self-sacrifice on the battlefield we are proud to record'.[74]

71 For more details of Ayles' trial, see C. Thomas, *Slaughter No Remedy: The Life and Times of Walter Ayles, Bristol Conscientious Objector* (Bristol, Bristol Radical Pamphleteer no. 36: 2016).
72 W.Ayles, *My Higher Duty to Conscience, Humanity and God* (NCF and ILP: c 1916).
73 M. C. Tothill, *Toleration or Persecution (*Manchester, National Labour Press: 1916).
74 Tothill, 'War and the Social Order'.

Mabel's depth of commitment to freedom of conscience and peace led her to concentrate her efforts after 1916 on helping conscientious objectors. She took on the role of honorary secretary of the Bristol Joint Advisory Committee for conscientious objectors, a group established by the ILP. In the absence of men, who were imprisoned or sent to fight, roles such as this were often taken on by women.[75] In Bristol, for example, the secretary of the local branch of the No Conscription Fellowship was Alice Chappell. She lived in Bedminster with her husband, a print worker, who was secretary of the Bristol branch of the Socialist Labour Party, and was imprisoned as a conscientious objector.

Mabel's support for conscientious objectors took many different forms. One of her aims was to publicise the difficulties faced by COs who were in civil prison or military barracks. When the local paper refused to print letters about ill treatment she produced a number of leaflets as well as writing in the ILP paper *Bristol Forward*. By these means she drew attention to the fact that COs at Horfield Prison were subject to solitary confinement, a bread and water diet and the removal of Bibles. They were unable to communicate with their friends and could be forced to wear khaki.[76] Ernest Gilpin, an ILP member, wrote to her from a military barracks that 'I am in soldier's clothes now, but I am not a soldier.' Mabel commented: 'what is the reason of a man's being forced into Khaki after the court martial had sentenced him to a civil prison?'[77] She published lists of names, with short descriptions, to show how many men were COs, the varied backgrounds they came from and beliefs that they held.

She made similar points in a letter to the chairman of the Gloucester Appeals Tribunal, pleading the case of individual men who had been denied exemption from military service. Mabel must have thought carefully about her tactics. Although she commented that 'justice has gone astray', she was careful to recognise that the tribunals had a difficult task to perform and that in Bristol they had attempted to act justly and had given a great deal of time to each case. She ensured that the letter was signed by individuals from a range of 'respectable' backgrounds. They included the Quakers Marian Pease, Helen Sturge and Elizabeth Ellis Giles. Aged just over sixty Elizabeth

75 For example, Catherine Marshall, one of the pre-war leaders of the NUWSS, became secretary of the No Conscription Fellowship. For the roles played by women in Manchester, see A.Ronan, *Unpopular Resistance* (Manchester, North West Labour History Society, 2015).
76 Mabel Tothill, *Conscientious Objectors at Horfield* (Manchester, National Labour Press, nd); see also *What Every Bristol Man Should Know* (Manchester, National Labour Press, nd); 'It's a way they have in the army', *The Bristol Labour Forward*, July 1916.
77 Tothill, 'It's a way they have in the army'.

Giles was a widow who ran her husband's corn merchant business.[78] Other signatories were Arthur Rashleigh, vicar of St Agnes and member of the ILP and Church Socialist League and Arthur Girdlestone, clerk in Holy Orders, Fishponds who, with his wife Lucy, was to be active in the ILP in the early 1920s. The tone of her letter was praised by the chairman although he declined to act upon it.[79]

Alongside propaganda work Mabel also gave more practical assistance to conscientious objectors and their families. This was completely in tune with the hands on approach that she had adopted in her welfare and settlement work. Political and personal life were inextricably linked since her home at Rosemary Street was used as a centre from which to coordinate work on behalf of COs.

It was also a place where men could come to for advice and support. Roland Reinge and his brother Sidney, both COs, were arrested as absentees in December 1916 and released pending trial. Roland recalled later that:

We then paid a visit to 27 Rosemary Street to let Mabel Tothill know what had happened. She was a Quaker lady who devoted practically her whole time to the conscientious objectors and to whom I am deeply grateful...she came to live at Rosemary Street, a house adjoining the [Friends'] Meeting House premises when conscription was introduced. There, with the help of other pacifist women, an open and ever-friendly house was kept where objectors, irrespective of religious or political beliefs could go for information. A list of CO names and addresses was kept and, when the local Tribunal sat, a number of sympathisers would always be in attendance to give support and carefully watch the procedures and attitudes of the Tribunal members'.[80]

78 Elizabeth Giles' address was 124 Hampton Road. Born in Yorkshire in 1854, she married Samuel Giles, a corn merchant and baker, in 1875. By 1881 they were living in Bath where he ran his business under the name Coleby and Giles. He died in 1894 and by 1901 his widow was living in Clifton. In 1911 she had moved to Westbury Park. Information from ancestry.com.

79 Letter from Mabel Tothill to the chairman of the Gloucester Appeals Tribunal, 14 June 1916 and his response, 16 July 1916, Gloucester Record Office, D570/3/1 and D570/3/3.

80 R.Reinge (CO/078), Liddle Collection, University of Leeds Special Collection, quoted in Pearce, 'Identifying war resister communities', p.10. See also the report about Elizabeth Hutchinson, a Quaker and friend of Mabel's, who met two men at the house who were waiting to go before the tribunal. She invited them to stay at her cottage where they did decorating for her. She was then summonsed for employing men who were absent without leave, *Western Daily Press,* 2 December 1916.

27 Rosemary Street, Mabel Tothill's home from which she organised the Joint Advisory Committee for Conscientious Objectors.

Mabel was well aware of the psychological as well as physical damage suffered by imprisoned men and their families. COs were often moved at short notice, leaving their families anxious about their whereabouts. Mabel used 'watchers' who stood outside Horfield Prison to report when a prisoner was moved. She then made sure that this information was passed on to their families as quickly as possible, often writing to them on a daily basis.

Prison visiting was a crucial part of her work since it enabled her to check on the welfare of prisoners and to attempt to improve their morale. In writing to the Gloucester Appeals Tribunal she noted how solitary confinement, a narrow cell with nothing to read and nothing to do, a diet of bread and water and 'perpetual attempts to persuade or coerce' men to submit had worn down the resistance of some.[81] Prison visiting was a key activity for the Society of Friends and Mabel was in touch with the central Visitation of Prisoners' Committee. It was reported that she had visited Princetown with a minute from the Bristol Quarterly Meeting to get a more

81 Letter to Chairman of the Tribunal, 14 June 1916, D570/3/1.

sympathetic response from the governor towards visitors.[82] She travelled to prisons all over the country to visit Bristol COs, including Ipswich, Winchester and Pentonville.[83] On one occasion she visited Wormwood Scrubs to see Ernest Gilpin, a Bristol ILP member. She found out that he had seen another CO, Eric Crompton. Although he had not been able to speak to him he had found that he was in good spirits. Mabel then immediately wrote to Eric's father to let him know.

Mabel was helped in her work by other pacifist women, including Alice Chappell, who also visited prisoners in Horfield, and Gertrude A. Giles who signed letters on her behalf when she was absent from home. Gertrude, a Quaker and daughter of Elizabeth Giles, had matriculated from London University at Duncan House, Clifton and worked at different times as a governess and then teacher.[84] Mabel also worked closely with other ILP women who formed a fund raising committee to help the men and their families. One of the committee, for example, was Miss Manning, secretary of the Bristol Women's Labour League and an ILP ward secretary of St Paul's.[85] Families of COs needed financial support since wives could be left with children to look after on very little income. But Mabel was also aware of the need of children to have fun and organised holidays and other amusements for them.[86]

The range of support that Mabel gave to COs provides us with a flavour of the intensity of peace work in this period. She was a single woman, but for married women activists there were the added personal anxieties that came when husbands were imprisoned. Annie Townley, Hannah Higgins and Bertha Ayles all had small children to look after and must have suffered from financial worries. Bertha Ayles, whose son was only three when her husband was imprisoned, was appointed organising secretary for the ILP on £2/10/- a week.[87] It was Annie Townley, however, who did the work and the payment was rescinded when Walter was released. Annie often accompanied Bertha on visits to Walter in prison, which served two purposes. She was able to give Bertha personal support and also discuss politics and the progress of the branch with Walter.

82 Visitation of Prisoners' Committee, Minute Book, April 19 1917, Friends Library, London.
83 Letter to Ernest Batten, a CO from Old Sodbury, who was doing agricultural work in East Anglia, June 1918, in Suffolk Record Office, Bury St Edmunds, HC502/182.
84 Gertrude Adele Giles was born in 1881, the fourth of six children of Elizabeth and Samuel Giles. In 1931 she married Joseph Dare from Hitchin who was a road and sewage contractor. In 1939 they lived in Brecon Road Bristol. Ancestry.com.
85 Bristol ILP Branch minutes, 16 January 1916.
86 Email from Cathy Dyer about her grandfather, Alfred Ernest James, 24/12/2016.
87 Bristol ILP Branch minutes, 27 September 1916.

As the war drew to a close many conscientious objectors were still imprisoned. Mabel Tothill played a key role in organising a meeting at the Kingsley Hall to call for their release. Letters of support came from different groups, including religious leaders, her friend Helen Sturge, a suffragist and member of the Women's International League, and Luke Bateman, the Labour candidate for Bristol East. Mabel seconded a resolution, moved by W. G. Brown, chairman of the Trades Council, calling on the Prime Minister to declare a political amnesty and to release all men who were in prison because of their religious and political convictions. She thought it was a pity that their own country, in its hour of triumph, had a lower base than Germany, a country they were supposed to despise, which had already opened the doors of its prisons.[88] It was not until later in 1919, however, that all COs were finally released.

Support for conscientious objectors was clearly the focus of Mabel Tothill's life and work for the last two years of the war. Nonetheless, she still found time to promote peace in other ways and had not lost sight of the importance of socialist politics for improving the lives of working-class men and women. With so many men fighting or in prison, women had to take on more prominent roles within the ILP. Annie Townley became chair of the branch when Walter Ayles was imprisoned and carried out much of his organising work as well as visiting him regularly in prison with his wife Bertha.[89] Mabel chaired numerous ILP meetings and continued as chair of the Bristol Peace Council. The Council welcomed the Leeds Convention of June 1917 when delegates from all branches of the labour movement met to acclaim the setting up of workers' councils in Russia. Stephen White has argued that support was given largely because it was hoped that this would pave the way for a speedy end to the war and a negotiated peace.[90] This was certainly Mabel Tothill's hope. She thought the first Russian Revolution was full of great possibilities for peace and for establishing international relations based on good will and cooperation.[91]

Such views were now becoming far more mainstream within the Labour Party as well as the ILP. In July 1917 a meeting called by the local committee, acting on behalf of the Provisional Committee of Workers and Soldiers, attracted delegates from 103 labour, cooperative, socialist and other organisations to consider the reconstruction of society on socialist

88 *WDP*, 2 December 1918.
89 Bristol ILP Branch minutes, AGM 22 April 1917–she is thanked for all her work in keeping the branch going.
90 Stephen White, 'Soviets in Britain: the Leeds Convention of 1917', *International Review of Social History*, XIX (1974).
91 *WDP*, 2 June 1917.

principles. Mabel was on the platform along with T. C. Lewis, secretary of the Trades Council, who shared her views on women's suffrage, peace and conscientious objection. A resolution was passed, with some dissent, supporting a charter of liberties to give complete political and social rights to all men and women. Mabel moved another resolution in favour of the coordination of working-class activity and in support of peace, which was carried 84 to 2.[92]

War and Women's Suffrage

During the same period there was a revival of activity around the question of women's suffrage. The government had raised concerns early in the war that men fighting for their country would be unable to vote when they returned. Some were disenfranchised because they had been away from home for too long. Others did not fulfil the property qualification. A Speaker's Conference was set up in 1916 to consider franchise reform. The conference made its recommendations in January 1917. It was proposed that women over 30 who were local government electors, or were married to one, should be given the vote. It was still not certain that this would be incorporated in the Bill and therefore women's suffrage groups began to campaign for their inclusion.

The East Bristol WSS held a meeting to support this campaign. Mabel Tothill was in the chair and reminded the audience that they had held no meetings for some time and had not broken from the electoral truce. But the government had re-opened the question. She was supported by Mr T. C. Lewis. He expressed his disappointment that the terms on which women were to be enfranchised were not those 'for which we stand' but urged the Government to introduce a Bill including women without delay. Mrs Mary Stocks from the executive of the NUWSS argued in similar terms that 'half a loaf was better than no bread'.[93]

The municipal vote was also affected by the proposals for franchise reform, but it was still not settled as to whether married women would be included in their own right. Annie Townley, secretary of the East Bristol WSS, played her part in supporting the campaign for married women's inclusion, led by NUWSS executive member Eleanor Rathbone. She sent resolutions to numerous labour organisations urging them to support the amendment which would include married women as local voters. The amendment was successful.

92 *WDP*, 30 July 1917.
93 *Common Cause* , 16 March 1917.

At the beginning of 1918 the East Bristol WSS had started election work in earnest and was still inextricably linked with the candidature of Walter Ayles. The key activities were registration work and Labour propaganda. When Annie Townley suggested that there should be a shop in Bristol to provide a focal point for this work her proposal was accepted. She was given power to start a fund and the shop was opened at 8 Cobden Street, which had long been a meeting place for the Bristol East ILP.[94] It was decided to merge the Tuesday afternoon meetings of the East Bristol WSS with those of the East Bristol Labour Party and suffrage supporters continued to be the mainstay of these meetings. There was still reluctance on the part of the NUWSS executive to release funds to help this campaign and they regarded East Bristol as a liability. Mary Stocks was successful, however, in moving a resolution of support for Walter Ayles, claiming that he was 'an out and out supporter of women's suffrage and would be a conscientious candidate on behalf of all women's questions.'[95]

For the time being, however, Walter Ayles and many other ILP activists remained in prison and it was left to the women to take the lead on registration work and propaganda. Annie Townley in particular addressed over fifty meetings. She was elected as agent for Walter Ayles by the East Bristol Labour Party and had been helping to set up other local Labour Parties in the constituency.

Women and the ILP in the aftermath of war

As noted above, Mabel Tothill, Annie Townley and other socialist women worked with Quakers, radical liberals and feminists in the cause of peace, as they had done before the war in the campaign for women's suffrage. Nonetheless, their approach as socialists could be different. They showed some impatience, for example, with the Women's International League which, at a national level, could be seen as rather unadventurous in its methods, and as failing to appeal to working-class women. This led ILP women to look for ways to involve working-class women in calling for a negotiated peace by tapping into their concerns with homes, family and work. It was planned to hold a Women's Peace Crusade in 1917 in which demonstrations would take

---

94 For example, those interested in registration work and canvassing were urged to meet at 8 Cobden Street, St George, before the war. *Labour Leader*, 2 July 1914.
95 *Common Cause* , 21 June 1918.

place in towns and cities throughout the country.[96] Annie Townley organised the Bristol contribution. She carried out a week's mission work to publicise the Crusade and called on other organisations to give support.[97]

Many members of the WIL were involved in other organisations which Mabel Tothill and Annie Townley kept away from. The most significant of these was the Bristol Training School for Women Patrols and Police, an initiative of the National Union of Women Workers (NUWW). The NUWW had been set up at the end of the nineteenth century to bring together women of all shades of opinion who were involved in social questions and social work. Many of Mabel's Quaker friends from the WIL, including Rosa Pease and Elizabeth and Helen Sturge, were on the committee, while Marianne Hill was the chair. They worked here alongside conservative women such as Emily Smith and Lilian Meade King who were committed patriots. The aim of the patrols was to 'safeguard wholesome recreation' and to promote 'a higher standard of self- control' in young women.[98] What started as an attempt to protect young women, however, could very quickly turn into middle-class control and policing of working-class behaviour, which ILP socialists would have found unpalatable.

Nonetheless, Mabel Tothill and Annie Townley's joint membership of the WIL and the ILP did ensure that the two groups remained close, especially in the volatile period following the ending of the war. They acted together, for example, over famine relief in Europe and the raising of money to buy teats for babies in Germany. The Bristol WIL passed resolutions in favour of self-government for India, the release of political prisoners and against continuing the blockade of Germany, all of which were supported by the ILP. The two groups were so close at this stage that in November 1919 the Bristol WIL agreed to support the Labour Party candidate and ILP member, Luke Bateman, at the next general election.[99] This support had to be withdrawn, however, when the national executive declared it to be against League policy.

It was in this brief period after the war, when there was uncertainty about daily life and the cost of living, that women, and some men, came

96 J. Liddington, 'The Women's Peace Crusade', in *Over Our Dead Bodies: Women Against the Bomb*. D. Thompson (ed.) (London, Virago: 1983). *The Women's Peace Crusade 1917-18: Crusading Women in Manchester and East Lancashire* (Manchester, Manchester Metropolitan University: 2017).
97 Bristol ILP Branch minutes, EC 5 September, 1917.
98 Annual Report Bristol Training School for Women Patrols and Police, 1916, 1917, p.10, Bristol Reference Library.
99 *WDP*, 26 November 1919.

together across political parties to draw attention to 'domestic issues'.[100] There were, for example, campaigns over the high price of milk and also over the need for a municipal lodging house for women. At the same time women highlighted the suffering of women and children in other European countries. Joint meetings continued to be held over specific issues. In November 1920, for example, a meeting was called at the Friends' Meeting House to protest about coercion and violence in Ireland and the importance of self-determination. Among those present were Mabel Cross, honorary secretary of the Bristol NUWSS and her husband, both of whom were active in the Liberal Federation, the Quaker Marianne Burrow Hill, Luke Bateman and Mabel Tothill. Mabel read out a letter from the Labour councillor J. Inskip, who was anxious to promote a spirit of reconciliation and a resort to peaceful negotiation.[101]

On the other hand, socialist women such as Mabel Tothill and Annie Townley increasingly emphasised that it was the Labour Party that offered the greatest hope for improving the lives of working-class men and women. At one election meeting Mabel claimed that 'housing problems were a disgrace to the city. If they cared for a better world and the future of the younger generation they must alter things' and vote for Labour councillors.[102]

This hope for a better world was shared by other women of her class and generation. Edith Picton-Turbervill, for example, who came from a well-connected Conservative family and who had been active in the Young Women's Christian Association, joined the Labour Party in 1919. She believed that it was 'in harmony with Christian thought and ethics' and declared that she voted Labour because 'the Party does its thinking in human terms'.[103] Now that some women had gained the parliamentary vote, and many more women could vote in local elections, women's organisations emphasised the importance of women standing for elected positions so that they could exert influence and make a difference. Some women stood for Parliament, including Edith Picton-Turbevill, who was elected as a Labour MP in 1929. Mabel's ambitions were more modest, but she did take the decision to stand for election to Bristol City Council.

100 K.Hunt, *Staffordshire's War* (Stroud, Amberley Publishing: 2017), p.142.
101 *WDP*, 4 November 1920.
102 *WDP*, 21 October 1921.
103 A.V. John, *Rocking the Boat: Welsh Women Who Championed Equality, 1840-1990* (Cardigan, Parthian: 2018), p.153.

Candidate for Bristol City Council

In 1919 Mabel's name was put forward to the Labour Party for inclusion on a list of municipal candidates and it was accepted.[104]

She would have preferred Redcliffe ward but was selected to contest St Paul's, a winnable seat in a working-class area where she was well known. This in itself is significant. Women often faced difficulties in being selected as candidates in the first place, let alone in seats where there was a possibility of success. If they were known peace campaigners then it could be even more difficult. Selina Cooper, a Lancashire suffragist, was initially chosen by the Nelson ILP to stand for Whitefield Ward but then her name appeared to slip from the list. Her biographer Jill Liddington suggests that her feminist and anti-war views would have told against her in a right-wing Catholic ward.[105] Hannah Mitchell, a suffragette, peace campaigner and socialist in Manchester claimed that despite being nominated by the ILP she was turned down for a seat by the local Labour Party after the war because 'I was too well known as a keen feminist, and, as they put it, "not amenable to discipline"'.[106]

This draws our attention to the importance of local structures, both of the Labour Party and of the electorate, in explaining whether women were chosen as candidates. In Bristol the ILP had been one of the largest branches in the country before the war. The trade union movement was not as strong as in many other cities, and the ILP dominated the Labour Representation Committee and the Trades Council. Although ILP membership fell during the war it had an effective ward organisation. This meant that it was able to reassert its position within the local Labour Party structure, in particular in East Bristol, once peace had been declared.[107] Mabel had become well known in Labour circles during the war. Her peace activities brought her closer to some members of the labour movement, in particular T. C. Lewis of the Trades Council, and she had attended Labour Party meetings as a representative from the ILP.

There were tensions, however, between the Labour Party and the ILP and also within the ILP itself, in particular between the Central Bristol branch and the East Bristol branch. Walter Ayles had been appointed as organiser by the former and both Annie Townley and Mabel Tothill were active in the Central group. The two branches often appeared reluctant to work together

104 Bristol ILP Branch minutes, 25 June and 16 July 1919.
105 Liddington, *The Life and Times of a Respectable Rebel*, p.299.
106 H. Mitchell, *The Hard Way Up. The Autobiography of Hannah Mitchell, Suffragette and Rebel*, G. Mitchell (ed.) (London, Virago: 1977, first published 1968), pp.194-5.
107 This point is made by R. Whitfield, 'The labour movement in Bristol, 1910-39', unpublished PhD thesis, University of Bristol, 1979, pp.161-2.

VOTE FOR
Mabel C. Tothill
The Labour Candidate.

Printed and Published by Bristol Printers, Ltd.,
Stratton Street St. Pauls.

An election poster from 1919.

and in 1918 the East Bristol branch chose Luke Bateman, who had trade union financial support, to be its Parliamentary candidate instead of Walter Ayles. Ayles was still in prison and there were issues about finance for the campaign. On his release Walter Ayles was selected as candidate for Bristol North, despite concerns from the National Administrative Council of the ILP that this would split the Party's resources. Luke Bateman was very supportive of Ayles during this difficult time and argued that it would help rather than hinder both of them if they were fighting adjoining constituencies.[108] In the 1922 election neither was successful, but in 1923 Walter Baker won Bristol East for Labour and Walter Ayles was successful in Bristol North.

Despite these difficulties ILP activists were a significant force in the local Labour Party in the early 1920s. Most officers were drawn from the ILP. In 1920 Walter Ayles and Annie Townley were chairman and vice-chairman respectively of the Bristol Labour Party and Mabel Tothill was a delegate to the Labour Party's executive committee.[109] Out of 16 Labour Party councillors in 1919, 12 were members of the ILP. Annie Townley was appointed in 1919 as a woman organiser for the Labour Party in the South West. She became a key figure, therefore, in the local party although, as a paid employee, she was at times constrained in her actions and could no longer give all her energies to the ILP.[110]

Mabel Tothill, Annie Townley, Hannah Higgins, Bertha Ayles and many other ILP women were part of a 'suffrage generation'. This helped to shape their political identity and approach after the war.[111] They thought the best hope for change in women's lives was through the mixed-sex Labour Party, even if compromises had to be made when questions of gender equality threatened to disrupt Party loyalty or the interests of male workers. But they also did their best to highlight the specific needs of women and were sensitive to the fears and desires of the woman in the home. At one of her campaign meetings Mabel argued that women should be elected rather than co-opted onto public bodies because there was an intimate connection between many matters to be dealt with by the council and the home. More nursery schools were needed so that 'the children of workers should be fully equipped for the battle of life'.[112]

108 Joint meeting of Bristol East and Bristol ILP branches, Bristol ILP Branch minutes, EC 9 July 1919.
109 Bristol ILP Branch minutes, EC 12 March 1919.
110 For more information on women organisers see J. Hannam, 'Women as paid organizers and propagandists for the British Labour Party between the wars', *International Labor and Working-Class History*, 77, Spring (2010).
111 P. Graves, *Labour Women: Women in British Working-Class Politics, 1918-1939* (Cambridge, Cambridge University Press: 1994), pp.12-13.
112 *WDP*, 24 September 1919.

Her argument was in tune with that of other socialist women activists in Bristol. They thought it was essential to draw attention to the ways in which politics was relevant to home life. In the women's column in *Bristol Forward* Bertha Ayles wrote that women did not realise that 'politics touches the home life at all points and that whether women interfere in politics or not, politics is sure to interfere with them...as soon as she rises in the morning and strikes a match to light the fire she is taxed. When she makes her tea for breakfast again she is taxed. She cannot even have a cup of cocoa for lunch without the tax-gatherer again worrying her.'[113] For Annie Townley women's sections provided a space not just to become informed about political affairs but also to bring changes in women's personal lives. She argued that they enabled housewives to meet together in the afternoon and to share their problems–many of which were overcome when realising that others had the same problems and that they could talk them through, and 'where for an hour she can feel the sense of responsibility as a citizen'.[114]

They tried to demonstrate why working-class women should be represented on the council and other relevant groups, and also to encourage working-class women themselves to take an interest in political affairs.[115] For example, at a special meeting held in 1923 Mabel Tothill, Lilian Pheysey, a Labour councillor, Annie Townley and the Labour Guardian, Mrs Batt, all spoke on the need for more women to stand for election to the Town Council and the Board of Guardians.[116]

Mabel Tothill's campaign in St Paul's in 1919 drew support from members of the ILP and the broader labour movement. At one meeting the chair claimed that they were not only anxious that St Paul's should return a Labour candidate but that 'they should be the pioneers in sending a woman to represent the electors on the City Council'. Reverend Girdlestone, A.E.Cannington and Annie Townley, all from the ILP, spoke in favour of the candidate. Annie Townley also read a letter of support from Ernest Bevin, the trade union leader, regretting that he could not be there to speak. Mabel herself began by asking the question, 'What had Liberals ever done?' She framed her answer within Walter Ayles' programme for municipal socialism, claiming there were no houses and that schools were overcrowded. There had been no attempt to municipalise the trams. Using an argument that appears just as relevant today she claimed that the council would let the Tramways

113 *Bristol North Forward*, February 1922.
114 *West Bristol Labour Weekly*, 24 September 1926.
115 See, for example, Bertha Ayles in *Bristol North Forward*, February 1922.
116 *WDP*, 20 September 1923.

Company put trams into Avonmouth and then at a future date would pay a lot to buy them back.[117]

Mabel was not successful in gaining election in 1919. Her opponent Alfred Strong, the son of an owner of a local engineering firm, made much of his working-class roots and the fact that he grew up in the locality. He had also been a member of the local munitions committee and of Bristol's Volunteer regiment during the war. It is unclear whether Mabel's pacifist stance made a difference to the voters. The *Bristol Guardian*, a paper supporting local ratepayers, was especially critical of conscientious objectors and their supporters. For example, it featured many cartoons that lampooned Walter Ayles for being unpatriotic.

It is not surprising, therefore, that the paper was critical of Mabel's candidature. One editorial noted that 'Miss Tothill, who was so busy during the war on behalf of men of military age who did not want to serve their country', was a candidate. 'Her opinions, being extreme, are angular, so that her presence in the social movement has been known to produce a sense of discomfort'.[118] On the other hand the *Western Daily Press* did not refer to her stand on the war and described her as 'a lady whose name is well known for her advanced opinions and good social work'. The paper claimed that 75% of the electors who voted in the ward were women, but complained that overall the electors showed great apathy and that the average turnout in the city was 33%.[119]

In St Paul's the number of eligible electors had increased threefold since 1912 but the turnout had only doubled. After her defeat Mabel was put forward by Labour councillors to become a member of the Education Committee. J. J. Milton, an ILP councillor, pointed out Mabel's reputation as a social worker and that she was a member of the University Extension movement. In proposing her, Alderman Parsons claimed that 'women are especially useful in education work'. The two other women on the committee were from the Conservative and Liberal parties and he argued that this would add some balance. Alderman Davies disagreed and claimed that the Labour Party had its fair share of representation already. On this occasion, therefore, Mabel was turned down.[120]

117 *WDP*, 31 October 1919.
118 *Bristol Guardian*, 18 October 1919.
119 *WDP*, 24 September 1919.
120 *WDP*, 11 November 1919.

THE ALDERMANIC VACANCY.

MR. BRISTOL: "Go away, we only want patriotic citizens!"
(See "Notes for Local Ratepayers.")

A cartoon from the *Bristol Guardian*, November 1921.

The first 'lady' councillor

In the meantime the ILP was still keen to get Mabel onto the council. Her name was put forward in April 1920 for Easton ward where Walter Ayles had been a member since 1912. The Party did not have long to wait. One month later Mabel finally entered the council unopposed. She took the seat of A. A. Senington who had been elevated to the aldermanic bench. She received congratulations from women's groups, including the Bristol South Association of Women Liberals and the National Federation of Women Teachers whose annual conference was being held in Bath.[121]

Her election as the first woman councillor was mentioned only briefly in most of the local press. It was the *Bristol Guardian* that provided the most extensive comments. The paper was so concerned about the 'menace' posed to ratepayers by socialists, and so critical of pacifists, that it was also motivated to write about them. The report of Mabel's election was headlined 'Enter a woman councillor' and it was noted that the Labour Party had scored a point in getting a woman elected for the council.[122] The *Guardian* provided a lengthy report about her first day on the council which was ambivalent in tone. It informed readers that when she entered the lobby she was greeted by a well known Corporation official who 'expressed the hope that she would keep the *naughty* boys around her in order'. It then went on to describe her appearance in neutral terms. 'The new councillor, we may inform our lady readers, was dressed in a neat grey coat and skirt, and wore a fancy straw hat with a blue ribbon. She carried a small attaché case. And took her seat with her Labour colleagues in the far right hand corner'.[123] She was introduced by Alderman Sheppard and was loudly cheered when she took her seat for the first time.[124] The Guardian, however,

Mabel Tothill, 1920.

121 *WDP*, 20 May and 26 May 1920.
122 *Bristol Guardian*, 22 May 1920.
123 *Bristol Guardian*, 12 June 1920.
124 *Portsmouth Evening News*, 9 June 1920.

could not resist undermining her with the comment that 'Miss Tothill, who wore a *simpering* smile, followed the debates with evident earnestness'.[125]

Mabel was only a councillor for eighteen months but while there she was active in proposing motions on topics ranging from housing to proportional representation.[126] The Labour Party was in a minority on the council and therefore Mabel suffered the same frustrations as her male colleagues in getting support for reforms that she wanted to pursue. On the other hand her position on the council did enable her to raise issues that might otherwise have not been aired. Her support for proportional representation was perhaps unusual. Her concern was that there were powerful minorities who were not represented and the single transferable vote would give every side a chance. Otherwise they might turn away from constitutional to other methods. She also hoped that it would lead to more contests at a municipal level.[127]

Mabel's main concerns, however, were housing and education and she pursued these both inside and outside the council. Bristol had an acute housing shortage after the war and the council received numerous deputations from Labour and Liberal groups, including one from working women, demanding more municipal housing.[128] Meetings were called as part of a housing campaign in the city and both Mabel Tothill and Walter Ayles were among the regular speakers.[129]. Mabel also moved a resolution at the ILP annual conference in 1920 that called on the Government to assume possession and control of all building materials and to give assistance to local authorities to help them build new houses. She argued that the government should take responsibility for housing in the same way as it did for roads and sanitation since all were 'essential to the decent life of the people'. If they 'did not liberate the women from the bondage of struggling against dirt and bad conditions, they were wasting the life of their women'.[130]

She took up this theme on the council. In 1921 she moved a resolution instructing the Housing and Town Planning Committee to repair houses occupied by the working classes in line with the 1919 Housing and Town

125 *Bristol Guardian*, 12 June 1920.
126 C.Haskins, 'Elected women in local government in Bristol during the inter-war years', unpublished MA thesis, University of the West of England, 2001, p.11.
127 *WDP*, 14 April 1921.
128 M. Dresser, 'People's housing in Bristol, 1870-1939', *Bristol's Other History*, Ian Bild (ed.) (Bristol, Bristol Broadsides:1983).
129 See, for example, A Citizen's Meeting, called by the Bristol Housing Campaign, held at Bishopston Parish Hall, which was addressed by Reverend Griffiths, Walter Ayles, Mabel Tothill and J. Randall, the allotments organiser. *WDP*, 22 April 1920.
130 ILP Annual Conference Report 1920, p.126.

Planning Act. She requested the government to enable local authorities to acquire, at site value, houses and sites where demolition orders had come into operation.[131] Her motion was amended, however, so that it was referred to the Committee for further consideration. This tended to be the fate of other issues raised by Labour Party councillors.

Mabel usually made reference to the specific impact that social reforms could have on women's lives. This was most evident when she introduced the question of sanitary improvements for men and women in the city. She drew attention to the ways in which women's freedom to enjoy public life was hampered by the lack of facilities and that they often had to resort to going to public houses. On this occasion the *Bristol Guardian* was complimentary. It reported that the speech was 'well phrased' and that a difficult subject was 'debated by her in a delicate manner and received favourable comment'.[132] Nonetheless her proposal did come in for criticism from the local press as not being economical for ratepayers.[133] Again it was referred back to the relevant sub-committee for consideration, but was not acted upon.

Mabel's other key interest at this time was unemployment, which she pursued outside the council. She joined with other members of the Fellowship of Reconciliation, including Walter Ayles and Lucy Cox, a young schoolteacher from Keynsham who had joined the ILP during the war, in signing a letter to the press on the subject.[134] They called on Christians to oppose an economic system that depended on a margin of unemployment and challenged the church to say whether its stand was 'God and Humanity' or 'Mammon and Charity'. The message of the letter was entirely in keeping with Mabel's views–that there should be practical schemes against unemployment, which only the Labour Party had put forward, and that all economic matters were also spiritual, since unemployment destroyed the body, dulled the mind and enfeebled character.[135]

Mabel followed this up by her own letter to the press. She focussed on the difficulties faced by unemployed women who were pressurised into

131 Bristol City Council Minute Book, 9 November 1921 to 31 October 1922.
132 *Bristol Guardian*, 16 October 1920.
133 *Bristol Evening News*, 12 October 1920; *WDP* 13 October 1920.
134 Lucy Cox was also a pacifist during the war, was Walter Ayles' election agent in the early 1920s and was active in the ILP at a regional level. She married the general secretary of the Labour Party, James Middleton, in 1936 and was elected MP for Plymouth Sutton in 1945. For more information, see J. Hannam, 'Middleton, Lucy Annie (1892-1983), Labour MP and socialist propagandist', in K. Gildart, D. Howell and N. Kirk (eds), *Dictionary of Labour Biography Volume XI*, (Houndmills, Palgrave Macmillan: 2003).
135 *WDP*, 14 March 1921. Walter Ayles was chairman and Lucy Cox secretary of the Bristol Fellowship of Reconciliation.

taking positions in domestic service. She believed that their unwillingness to do so needed some explanation. Mabel argued that it was not the nature of the work itself, which could be pleasant and interesting, that put off young women, but the long hours, the lack of freedom and the inferior position into which servants were placed. If domestic work were put on a proper basis it would get recruits.[136]

The Bristol ILP at this time linked together unemployment and foreign policy. A conference was held on the topic at the Kingsley Hall, chaired by Mabel. She pointed to the ways in which unemployment was exacerbated by the aftermath of war since the resurgence of nationalism over internationalism paralysed trade. The opportunity was taken at the meeting to pass a resolution to alter the provisions of the treaty of Versailles.[137]

Mabel's experience of hostility as a peace activist during the war must have helped her to deal with negative comments when she was a councillor. All socialists were criticised for supporting policies that would increase the burden on the rate payer. Mabel, however, suffered more personal attacks because of her earlier support for conscientious objectors and also her gender. Comments often related to her marital status, age and attractiveness. When she first took her seat the *Guardian* published a cartoon in which the lady councillor was depicted as a shepherdess, but the poem underneath made it clear that there was no comparison between 'Miss T and this Arcadian queen'.[138]

When Lilian Maud Pheysey, a mother of eight, was elected as a Labour Party councillor a few months later, the paper claimed that she would be 'a companion for Miss Tothill who has so far seemed a bit lonely in the Labour corner of the Council Chamber...the first named represents the married woman, the second the "maries".[139] Just the insertion of one word could make a serious proposal appear lightweight. When she gave a talk that suggested that town planners should consider creating an environment that would provide beauty for all, Mabel was described as an 'idealist'. It was admitted that she had come up with 'a nice *little* programme', but 'who foots the bill for Miss Tothill's *Arcadia*'.[140]

136 *WDP*, 20 August 1921.
137 *WDP*, 26 September 1921.
138 *Bristol Guardian*, June 12 1920.
139 *Bristol Guardian*, 25 September 1920.
140 *Bristol Guardian*, 14 August, 1920. Italics added by author.

THE SHEPPARD AND THE SHEPHERDESS.

Our witty artist, "F. G. L.,"
Has drawn the shepherdess—and drawn her well—
Hush! no comparison exists between
Miss T. and this Arcadian queen!

A cartoon from the *Bristol Guardian*, June 1920.

A municipal contest

By the end of 1921 Mabel had to contest her council seat. In urging readers to vote against her, the *Guardian* described her again as an idealist and also questioned her authenticity. 'Miss Tothill has no claims really to pose as a representative of Labour, and apparently belongs to the latter-day phenomena, the leisured class, who have taken up the cause of Labour as a transient "cult". Labour has really nothing to gain from such; their ideas are impracticable and visionary'. In a later report she was described as a 'coadjutor' of Ayles and a 'pseudo-labour councillor'.[141]

141 *Bristol Guardian*, 29 October and 5 November 1921.

Mabel faced a conservative opponent, Horace Walker, a chocolate manufacturer from Sneyd Park. He described himself as a 'non- political candidate' and criticised the representation of class over political opinion. In an election meeting in Easton Mabel claimed that she wanted to get rid of class, but at the moment the working class were the largest group and had most claim to be represented. Referring to the coalition of Liberals and Conservatives she accused them of defeating Labour efforts to get better housing and of being afraid that their privileged position was in danger. She argued that the unemployed were suffering because of private ownership of land and property and described the housing problem of the city as a disgrace. She called again for better conveniences for women in the city, better schools, more accommodation in hospitals and for a women's lodging house.

Mabel was supported by A. A. Sennington and Walter Ayles, both of whom were councillors in Easton. Ayles accused Horace Walker of profiteering and of flaunting his cheque book in the face of the electors. He argued that it was businessmen who were responsible for inefficiency on the council and claimed that nothing had been said by Walker against the Labour Party or the endeavours of Mabel Tothill. She 'had been faithful to the working classes, and they must be faithful to her'.[142] This last comment could be taken to imply that some working–class voters were suspicious of her middle-class background. On the other hand she did have strong support from some quarters. An enthusiastic meeting of the Greenbank Co-operative Education Council discussed 'the good work done by Miss Tothill' as a member for Easton. The meeting passed a resolution pledging that the whole of the membership would do their utmost to support her.[143]

Mabel was not elected. The turnout was higher than in 1919–50%–and she polled 1434 votes, less than 200 behind her opponent. It is impossible to know whether her anti-war campaigning was responsible for this. Walter Ayles had held a seat in this ward since 1912 and had been elected again in 1919, soon after his release from prison. The electorate might have been affected by the claims that many of Mabel's proposals would raise rates, but then this position was common to all Labour Party councillors. In the post-war period of anti-Bolshevism she had also been accused of being a communist, which she strenuously denied, since communists proposed to use force to obtain their aims whereas she preferred to change ways of thinking.[144] It is perhaps interesting that Walter Ayles also failed to gain re-election to the council in the following year. He gained more votes than on previous occasions but lost

142 *WDP*, 21 October 1921.
143 *WDP*, 14 October 1921.
144 *WDP*, 25 October 1921.

by 300 to his opponent. Easton did not become a solidly Labour Party ward until 1925, after which all seats were held by the party until the 1980s.[145]

The Labour Party did remain supportive of Mabel's attempt to get back onto the council. She stood twice more in St Paul's, in 1923 and 1924 but was unsuccessful, losing by 300 and then 500 votes respectively. Both of her opponents had been councillors in the ward since before the war but they were beaten by Labour opponents in 1926 and 1927. As with Easton all seats were held by the Labour Party from 1925 until the 1960s. Again there is no evidence as to why Mabel was defeated or why she did not stand again after 1924.

Propagandist for the ILP and the Labour Party in the 1920s

Throughout most of the 1920s Mabel remained active in propaganda work for the ILP and the Labour Party. She chaired or spoke at meetings in support of Labour candidates – at one in favour of E. H. Parker in St Paul's she declared that the need for the Labour Party seemed even greater to her after her experience on the council : 'The rich had ruled for too long and if the Labour Party was not in power it was because workers had not put it there'.[146] At another, she praised the prospective candidate, Ruby Part, for the wide sympathies and experience that she had gained as an organiser for the Workers' Union while her membership of the Board of Guardians had given her an understanding of the workings of a large public body. Taking the opportunity yet again to draw attention to housing conditions in Bristol, she blamed the city council for not facing the problem years ago.[147]

Mabel attended and spoke at the large, annual labour May Day rallies up to at least 1927. She also spoke at Labour demonstrations in the city, including one on Durdham Down in June 1924 for Labour Women's Day when she was joined by Walter Ayles, Annie Townley and local Labour MPs.[148] She never lost her interest in women's social position and their role in Labour politics. When a conference of women organised by the Joint Women's Committee, representing the Women's Co-operative Guilds, the Labour Women's Sections and the Railway Women's Guilds was held at the Kingsley Hall she was amongst the participants. The aim of the Committee was to organise conferences, meetings and demonstrations to 'watch women's

145 S. Jordan, K. Ramsay and M.Woollard , *Abstracts of Bristol Historical Statistics. Part 3. Political Representation and Bristol's Elections, 1700-1997* (Bristol, University of the West of England: 1997), pp.79-83.
146 *WDP*, 20 October 1920.
147 *WDP*, 29 October 1921.
148 *West Bristol Labour Weekly*, 10 September 1926; *Labour Woman*, July 1924.

Meeting of the Women's Co-operative Guild, Methodist Central Hall, Old Market St. 1936

interests on local administrative bodies and to carry our propaganda in the interests of the Co-operative and Labour movement'. Bertha Ayles presided and was supported by Mabel and councillor Lilian Pheysey.[149]

Issues relating to gender inequalities that caused tensions within the Labour Party at a national level, in particular access to birth control and support for family allowances, were seldom raised at a local level in Bristol in the 1920s. The party was in a weak position on the council and men and women worked together to pursue welfare reforms that were less controversial.

Mabel remained active within the ILP itself, attending many conferences as a delegate, including the South West Divisional Conference and the Annual Conference of the National ILP.[150] In 1921 she was elected as vice chair of the Bristol branch of the ILP with Annie Townley as chair. The two women alternated in chairing meetings until Annie Townley became too tied up with her work as a Labour Party organiser to continue. In 1922, therefore, Mabel became chair, a post she was to hold until at least 1924.[151] She represented the

149 *WDP*, 9 October 1924.
150 Bristol ILP Branch minutes, 15 February 1922 and 17 March 1920.
151 Bristol ILP Branch minutes, AGM 10 April 1921 and 23 April 1922 .

Bristol ILP on many other groups, including the Divisional Council of the ILP and the executive committee of the Bristol Labour Party, where she was elected as vice chair in 1921.[152] She was one of six ILP members, including Annie Townley and Lucy Cox, by then Walter Ayles' agent, who joined a new committee to devise work schemes to raise money to fund Walter Ayles' Parliamentary candidature in North Bristol.[153]

Education and Peace

Alongside her propaganda work for the ILP Mabel continued to pursue her lifelong commitment to promoting education for all. She was active in the Workers' Education Association, the Adult Schools movement and a new organisation, the Folk House, set up in 1919.

It had similar aims to the Settlement, providing a space to bring people of all classes together and offering an educational programme. Mabel was involved with the Bristol Folk House from the start. The first warden was a close friend, Paul Sturge, a Quaker who had been involved in the Adult School and the pre-war Barton Hill Settlement, helping to establish a boys club there.[154] His first wife died in the flu epidemic after the war and when he married again Mabel invited him to live in a maisonette that she owned at 12 Berkeley Square.[155] She kept in close touch with the family, staying for two days with them on a number of occasions before they left for London in 1935. She then visited them in Orpington in 1936 and again after the war in 1945.[156] Mabel was chair of the Folk House Council which was in financial difficulties by 1930. Nonetheless, Mabel was hopeful that they would get a grant from the Education Committee which would enable them to expand their educational and social work and to maintain a good relationship with other community centres.[157]

Mabel gave talks regularly for all these groups. She often linked together her main interests—education, peace, spirituality and the importance of beauty. When the WEA produced a circular for the elections which called for children to have more physical education, Mabel suggested an amendment so that it read 'if the physical training is of a non- military character'.[158] In similar vein, she complained at the weekly meeting of the Folk House

152 Bristol ILP Branch minutes, 15 March 1922 and 12 May 1920. *WDP*, 27 April 1921.
153 Bristol ILP Branch minutes, 15 March 1922.
154 Jennings, *Bristol University Settlement* (1971), p.14.
155 Personal information from Roger Sturge, son of Paul Sturge; Kelly's Directory for Bristol, 1923.
156 Visitor Book of Paul Sturge, by kind permission of Roger Sturge.
157 *WDP*, 3 February 1930.
158 *WDP*, 31 October 1919.

The Folk House, by Samuel Loxton, 1920.

Debating Society that the sum spent by the government on education was far smaller than that spent on the armed services.[159]

Her approach was always to seek reconciliation rather than the use of force. She was in the chair for a meeting of the Weston Super Mare Peace Society at the Friends Meeting House, to protest against the use of British troops in China. In 1927 there was civil war between Government troops and the Communist Red Army in China, which prompted the British Government to dispatch troops to protect the interests of British residents in Shanghai. Mabel moved a resolution calling on the government to stop the naval and military forces now on their way to China since, she argued, the landing of more troops would 'endanger the lives of foreign residents' and would 'create serious international disturbances in the whole East'.[160] Her belief in the importance of reconciliation could be applied to other areas of reform as well as to international affairs. Speaking to the WEA about penal reform, for example, she pointed to the need for public opinion towards prisoners to change and called for all notions of revenge to be put aside.

The importance of beauty was another theme of her talks. At a meeting of the College Green Adult School she emphasised that building houses and roads should not be at the expense of the beauty of the countryside. She

159 *WDP*, 19 February 1921.
160 *WDP*, 12 February 1927.

believed that there was great scope for municipal action to promote beauty and to provide the best drama, opera, music and cinema.[161] Her talk on 'The appeal through the eye' at the Folk House was more religious in tone. She argued that for most people the voice of God was heard through nature and that emotions were stirred through the glory of it. This was not always the case for town dwellers and therefore the common things in life should 'bear the stamp of beauty so they could bear a sacramental value'. All those connected with the Folk House should be given beauty and dignity so that they could appreciate 'Divine immanence'.[162]The importance of ensuring there was beauty and culture in working people's lives had long been a demand of 'new life socialism', while town planning that could enhance rather than destroy an attractive environment was an aim of the Garden Cities movement and the Kyrle Society, an organisation that had many members drawn from the suffrage movement.[163]

Mabel's financial assistance to causes she saw as important could be as crucial as her political work. In this she followed the example of other women of her class and generation. Single women in particular, who controlled their own resources, played an important part in contributing to the social and political life of their cities.[164] As well as her support for the pre-war Settlement Mabel also helped to finance the establishment of working girls' clubs and nurseries. In 1912, for example, she purchased a house in Hebron Road. This enabled the Old Girls' Society of Clifton High School to establish a new working girls' club when the old one had outgrown its premises. During the war, in 1916, she started the Friary nursery school and play centre, which was taken over by the Society of Friends in 1924, while in 1922 she contributed to a club for unemployed women and girls that was opened by the Mayoress in March.[165]

In the face of humanitarian crises Mabel joined with her Quaker friends in appealing for funds and donated money herself. She signed the appeal of the Bristol Society of Friends for famine sufferers in Russia along with Marian Pease, Helen Sturge and Monica Wills, and gave £100 to the cause.[166]

161 *WDP*, 11 August 1920.
162 *WDP*, 1 December 1920.
163 S. Rowbotham and J. Weeks, *Socialism and the New Life: The Personal and Sexual Politics of Edward Carpenter and Havelock Ellis* (London, Pluto: 1977). The Kyrle Society founded in London in 1875 by Miranda and Octavia Hill aimed to 'promote a sense of beauty and to stimulate pride in the domestic and civic life of the people' by preserving historic buildings and natural beauty in towns and cities. Bristol Kyrle Society, Annual Reports, 1908-13 and 1923-38.
164 M.Dresser (ed.), *Women and the City: Bristol 1373-2000* (Bristol, Redcliffe Press: 2016), p.111.
165 *WDP*, 29 December 1916 and 11 March 1922.
166 *WDP*, 2 November 1921.

Support for other causes must have been prompted by the involvement of old friends and colleagues. She gave donations of £50 and £20 respectively to the Winford Orthopaedic Hospital appeal for new buildings and the Bristol Crippled Children's Society. In both cases her colleague from the pre-war Civic League, Fanny Townsend, was chair of the relevant committees.[167]

The Folk House, the Sandford Women's Institute and the YHA

From 1927 onwards there is little evidence that Mabel Tothill remained active in either ILP or Labour Party politics. The local ILP, which had provided her with such a congenial space to pursue her interests, had changed. The group of friends with whom she had worked so closely and had shared a commitment to women's suffrage, peace and municipal socialism were no longer at the centre of the ILP in Bristol. Walter Ayles and Lucy Cox had left Bristol for London in 1924 to work for the No More War movement, and Bertha had gone with them, while Annie Townley now had to give a full time commitment to her work as a Labour Party organiser.

Mabel moved out of her Rosemary Street address after 1923 to live at Little Orchard, Sandford, in the parish of Winscombe. It was here during the 1930s that she continued to play a public role. She remained interested in education, peace and women's welfare, but pursued these concerns through different organisations. She was president of the Sandford Women's Institute, organising speakers and giving talks herself to other branches. On a more light-hearted note, she won many competitions for her brown eggs at the Winscombe WI annual show.[168] She also stood as one of nine candidates for Winscombe Parish Council in 1931.[169]

Mabel retained her interest in young people and education. She remained involved in the Folk House and also the WEA. Marian Pease was honorary treasurer of the Western Division of the WEA and Mabel paid an annual subscription of £1/1/- until the early 1940s.[170] She was a vice president of the regional Youth Hostel Association and was also a governor of Badminton School, Westbury on Trym. The ethos of the school was an exact fit with her interests—it believed in the League of Nations, sent pupils on trips abroad

---

167 *WDP*, 22 April 1925. Fanny Townsend was also on the Council of the University Settlement.
168 *WDP*, 3 May 1938; *Bristol Evening Post*, 1 April 1939.
169 *WDP*, 10 March 1931.
170 WEA Western Division Annual Reports, 1933-1947. Bristol Reference Library, B.3936. Mabel subscribed until 1943–the year after a Miss E. C. Tothill paid subs. Marian Pease, appointed as honorary treasurer in 1914, retained this position until 1940-1.

to foster an international outlook and educated girls in world affairs. One of its aims was to 'inculcate an ideal of service', something that had been a guiding principle of Mabel's own life.[171] At one speech day, for example, there were numerous prizes related to the League of Nations and awards for posters designed for Peace Week.[172]

Mabel also continued to think deeply about her religious views. Throughout her life her writings–whether articles that appeared in publications of the Society of Friends or reports that she had undertaken for various groups–came back to the theme of the responsibility of the individual, through personal service, to help to eliminate social problems, including poverty, unemployment and war, in order to 'help forward the Kingdom of God on earth'.[173] She was concerned to explore how Quakers in particular might leave Meetings concerned to 'be doing something, rather than being something' and to gain the realisation that the Kingdom was not simply 'a justly ordered world', but 'the abode of spiritual life'.[174]

Final Years

It is difficult to trace Mabel Tothill's life during and after the Second World War but she clearly remained interested in current affairs and was, of course, still committed to peace. She wrote a letter to the *Friend* supporting Marian Pease in her protest against bombing. Mabel pointed out how women and children were being killed and that only the ending of war could stop the 'insane slaughter'.[175]

She was intrepid enough to drive a car. As a young man Roger Sturge remembers Mabel lending her car to his father just after the war to visit his grandparents. He recalls that she was by then, to his eyes, a 'wizened old lady'.[176] In 1943 Gertrude Tothill moved from her Pembroke Road house and the two sisters auctioned both the house and its contents. Gertrude died in Guildford, aged 80, the following year.[177]

The final public reference to Mabel is an article that she wrote in the *Friends Quarterly Examiner* about the journal of Sarah Jane Luty of Cotham,

171 *More Memories of Bristol* (Bristol: True North Books, 2001).
172 *WDP*, 21 June 1937.
173 M.C.Tothill, 'Thoughts on the Queries', *Wayfarer*, vol 10, 12 January (1932); see also M. C. Tothill, 'Relation of Personal devotion to Social Services', *WDP*, 4 January 1924.
174 Mabel C. Tothill, 'From Fear to Wonder', *Wayfarer*, vol 15 no.5 May (1936).
175 *The Friend*, 16 July 1943.
176 Personal information, Roger Sturge.
177 *WDP*, 22 December 1943 and 29 July 1944.

written in 1928 under the title *Reminiscences of a Wandering Spirit*.[178] Sarah Luty died in 1946 aged 98 and Mabel remembered her as a familiar figure in the Quarterly meeting of Bristol and Somerset Friends. Plainly dressed in black with a white bonnet she seemed to be a re-incarnation of early Quakerism 'before conventionality and quietism had settled on it.' At some point Mabel moved back to Bristol to live at 3 Downside Road, Clifton. She died, aged 96, at Cossham Memorial Hospital on 26 September 1964 leaving an estate of £71,763.

Afterword

In her mid-seventies Mabel Tothill wrote a review of a memoir dedicated to her friend from Settlement days, Hilda Cashmore. In this she expressed what had been important in her own life. For her, the memoir demonstrated the importance of Hilda Cashmore's influence on others. It also showed the way for those who, 'wanting to be of service to the community, have not yet found how many channels are open to whatever they have learned to give'.[179] From the beginning of her adult life Mabel Tothill had sought ways to be of service to others. She was motivated by her Quaker faith and also her commitment to education, peace and women's rights which were shared by other women of her class and generation.

Where she differed from many of her radical liberal contemporaries, however, was by becoming involved in socialist politics. She was attracted by the municipal socialist programme of Walter Ayles and by the Christian principles which underpinned the politics of many in the Bristol ILP. She was committed to achieving change through constitutional means and to winning hearts and minds by appeals to a common humanity which she saw as compatible with the ILP. For Mabel, as for many other socialist women in the aftermath of war, it was socialist and labour politics that held the key to a better life for all.

A study of her life and work, therefore, can tell us a great deal about the different routes that individuals took on their journey towards an involvement in socialist and labour politics. It can also add to our understanding of the complex nature of ILP socialism in the early years of the twentieth century and its distinct local characteristics.

---

178 M. C. Tothill, 'Reminiscences of a Wandering Spirit', *Friends Quarterly Examiner*, vol.80, no. 319 1946, pp.164-8.
179 M. Pease ed. *Hilda Cashmore, 1876-1943* (Gloucester, J. Bellows: c 1944), reviewed in *The Friend*, 24 August 1945.